Leaders Congress

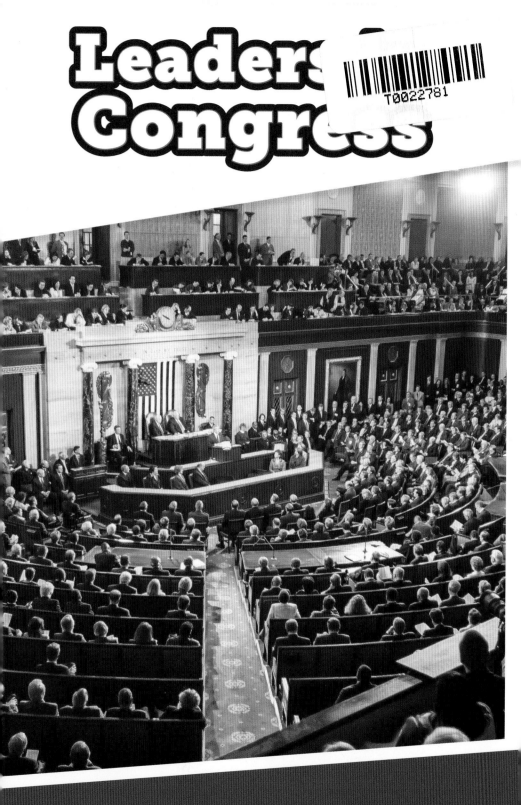

Mary Kate Bolinder

Reader Consultants

Brian Allman, M.A.
Classroom Teacher, West Virginia

Cheryl Norman Lane, M.A.Ed.
Classroom Teacher, California

iCivics Consultants

Emma Humphries, Ph.D.
Chief Education Officer

Taylor Davis, M.T.
Director of Curriculum and Content

Natacha Scott, MAT
Director of Educator Engagement

Publishing Credits

Rachelle Cracchiolo, M.S.Ed., *Publisher*
Emily R. Smith, M.A.Ed., *VP of Content Development*
Véronique Bos, *Creative Director*
Dona Herweck Rice, *Senior Content Manager*
Dani Neiley, *Associate Editor*
Fabiola Sepulveda, *Series Designer*

Image Credits: p12 Shutterstock/Aaron of L.A. Photography; p12 bottom Shutterstock/Pamela Au; p13 Shutterstock/Mark Reinstein; p14 Shutterstock/Tinxi; p15 Getty Images/Chip Somodevilla; p17 top Shutterstock/JL Images; p17 bottom Alamy/Imago History Collection; p18 Newscom/Kevin Dietsch - Pool via CNP/picture alliance/Consolidated News Photos; p19 Newscom/Michael Brochstein/Polaris; p20 Newscom/Yuri GRIripas/Reuters; p21 Library of Congress [LC-DIG-hec-25685]; p22 Getty Images/Bill Clark; p23 right Alamy/White House Photo; p25 top National Archives; p25 The White House; p29 Library of Congress [LC-DIG-hec-35354]; all other images from iStock and/or Shutterstock

Library of Congress Cataloging-in-Publication Data

Names: Bolinder, Mary Kate, author. | iCivics (Organization)
Title: Leaders in Congress / Mary Kate Bolinder.
Description: Huntington Beach,CA : Teacher Created Materials, 2022. |
  "iCivics"--Cover. | Audience: Grades 4-6 | Summary: "The president is
  not the only leader in Washington, DC. The United States Congress is
  filled with leaders from every state. These members in the Senate and
  the House of Representatives make laws for the country. With 535 members
  in all, they help things to run well. Find out more about the leaders in
  Congress who get the job done"-- Provided by publisher.
Identifiers: LCCN 2021054717 (print) | LCCN 2021054718 (ebook) | ISBN
  9781087615486 (paperback) | ISBN 9781087630595 (ebook)
Subjects: LCSH: United States. Congress--Leadership--Juvenile literature. |
  Political leadership--United States--Juvenile literature.
Classification: LCC JK1025 .B65 2022 (print) | LCC JK1025 (ebook) | DDC
  328.73/0762--dc23/eng/20211203
LC record available at https://lccn.loc.gov/2021054717
LC ebook record available at https://lccn.loc.gov/2021054718

5482 Argosy Avenue
Huntington Beach, CA 92649
www.tcmpub.com

ISBN 978-1-0876-1548-6

© 2022 Teacher Created Materials, Inc.

Table of Contents

Welcome to Capitol Hill

The White House is home to the president of the United States, but did you know there is another important white building in Washington, DC? It is the **Capitol**, a large building with a dome on top. Sometimes called Capitol Hill, it is home to the **Senate** and the **House of Representatives**. Together, they are known as **Congress**.

Congress is the **legislative branch** of the government. Congress has many responsibilities, but its main job is to make laws for the country.

The United States is a **democracy**. This means that the people of the United States elect their leaders. Members of Congress come from all 50 states. There are 535 elected members in all! With so many people in Congress, it can sometimes be hard for everyone to work together. What if everyone tried to talk at the same time? What if no one took turns or listened? It would be difficult to get anything done. That is why there are important leaders in Congress. There are special leaders in the House of Representatives. The Senate has its own leaders, too.

Come take a trip to Capitol Hill to learn more about the people who work there and how they help the country.

Jump into Fiction

Izzy and the Student Congress

Izzy woke up with butterflies in her stomach. Today was the big debate in Student Congress. All week, students in Izzy's class talked about where they wanted to go on the end-of-year class trip. The two choices were New York City and Washington, DC. This was a big decision, and Izzy was in charge of the debate. She might also have to cast a tie-breaking vote. There was just one problem—Izzy could not make up her mind.

"Hey, Izzy!" shouted Kyla as they walked into school. "Are you ready? I spent all night working on my speech. I can just see us walking down the streets of the Big Apple!" Kyla said as she linked arms with Izzy.

"Sure, Kyla," said Izzy. "NYC sounds great. But since I'm leading the Student Congress, you know I can't vote unless there's a tie. You need to convince the rest of the class, not me." The bell rang and the girls walked to their separate classrooms. "See you on the floor!"

Izzy took her seat next to her friend, Alex, as Mrs. Johnson took attendance. "Yo, Izzy," whispered Alex. "You have me on the schedule for the debate today, right?"

Izzy pulled the schedule of speakers out of her folder. "You're up after Kyla," said Izzy. "Then, we take a vote."

"I'm already packing my bags for Washington, DC!" said Alex. "This should be easy."

"I'm not so sure about that," replied Izzy. "Do you know who wants to vote on your side?"

Alex frowned. "I'll have to ask around."

At lunch, the whole class was buzzing about the Student Congress assembly that afternoon. Kyla and Alex walked from table to table, talking about why their choice was the best.

"I think NYC would be the best trip! We can see a Broadway show, walk through Central Park, or visit the Statue of Liberty," Izzy heard Kyla say.

At another table, Alex said, "There are so many cool museums, monuments, and parks in DC! Maybe we'll even see the president while we are there!"

At the Student Congress assembly that afternoon, Izzy called each representative to the stage. Kyla and Alex started the debate. There were chants of "NYC for you and me!" and "DC is the place to be!" Both representatives gave very convincing speeches. But who would win?

Finally, it was time for all the representatives to vote. Izzy tallied the votes. Ten votes for NYC . . . and ten votes for Washington, DC. It was a tie! Izzy would have to make the tie-breaking vote.

Which would she choose?

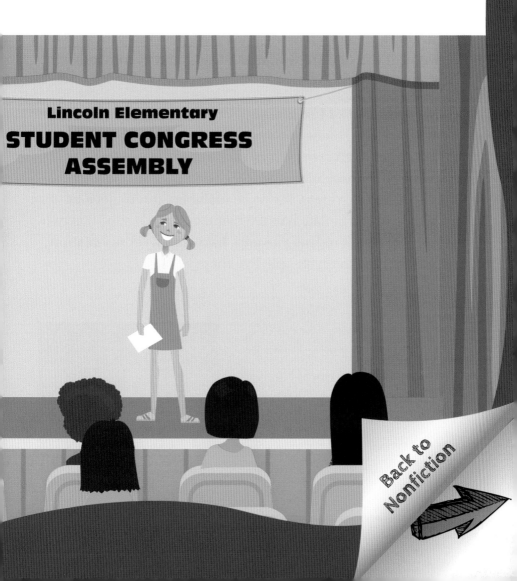

Lincoln Elementary
STUDENT CONGRESS ASSEMBLY

Back to Nonfiction

What Is Congress?

The government is made up of three parts. These parts are called *branches*. The president of the United States is the head of the executive branch. This branch carries out the laws. The legislative branch makes the laws. The judicial branch decides whether the laws are fair.

Congress is the legislative branch. It is divided into two parts: the House of Representatives and the Senate. A legislative branch that is split into two parts is called **bicameral**. Besides making laws, Congress has other powers. It can declare war, make taxes, and even remove the president from office!

Each member of Congress is elected by citizens of their own state. The House of Representatives has 435 members. The number of members from each state is based on population, or how many people live in a state. The more people living in a state, the more members it will have in the House. The Senate has 100 members. Each state has two **senators**, which means all states have equal representation no matter how many people live there.

Who's the Boss?

Each senator works for their entire state. Each representative works for one district in their state.

Executive   Legislative   Judicial

Congress

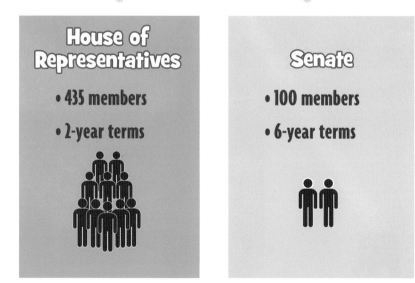

House of Representatives

- 435 members
- 2-year terms

Senate

- 100 members
- 6-year terms

Speaker of the House

Each member in the House of Representatives belongs to a party. But there aren't any balloons or cake in this party! A party is a group of people who share similar views on how the country should be run. The two biggest parties in the United States are the Democratic Party and the Republican Party. Both parties want what is best for their country. But they often times disagree.

The number 435 is an odd number. This means one party will have more members than the other in the House. There will not be a tie. The party with the most people in it is called the **majority**. The party with the fewest people in it is called the **minority**.

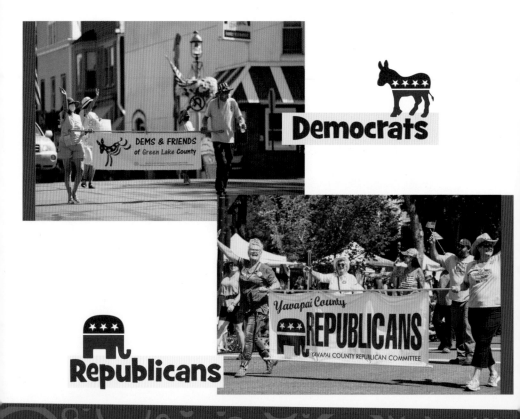

Democrats

DEMS & FRIENDS of Green Lake County

Yavapai County REPUBLICANS
YAVAPAI COUNTY REPUBLICAN COMMITTEE

Republicans

The **speaker of the house** addresses the representatives.

Often, members of each party have differing views. It can be hard for so many people to agree on the same things! This is why they chose a leader to help guide them. Representatives are elected to a two-year term in Congress. At the beginning of each new term, a member of the majority party is chosen as the leader of the House of Representatives. This leader is called the speaker of the house.

Double Duty

James K. Polk of Tennessee was the only person ever elected speaker of the house (in 1835) and president (in 1844).

What the Speaker Does

Can you guess what the speaker of the house does? You are right if you think the speaker of the house does a lot of talking! The speaker is called *Mister Speaker* or *Madam Speaker*. This person is the voice of the House. The speaker has been in Congress for many years before being chosen for this job. This person must understand all the rules of Congress and help others follow these rules. They must be able to convince people to cooperate. The speaker has many jobs and must be very organized! The speaker sets the schedule and tells people when they can speak. This person also assigns representatives to special committees and works with leaders in the Senate. The speaker of the house must manage more than 400 people when Congress is in session. Imagine being in charge of that many people!

The speaker of the house has another important role. If the president and the vice president are unable to serve, the speaker of the house becomes the president! This has never happened in the history of the United States.

Woman of the House

In 2007, Nancy Pelosi became the first female speaker of the house. She served in Congress for 20 years before she was elected speaker.

Representative Paul Ryan served as speaker of the house.

Floor Leaders

Congress is in session! It is time to get to work! Inside the Capitol building, there are two large rooms called *chambers*. This is where members of the House and the Senate meet. When members are in this room, they are said to be *on the floor*. The speaker of the house calls the House of Representatives to order. The daily schedule can begin.

What do senators and representatives do when they meet? Members of Congress work together to make fair laws for everyone in the United States. This is a big responsibility! When members of Congress want to talk about a new issue, they start a debate. A debate is when people from different parties discuss their different opinions about a topic. In the House, the speaker of the house chooses when and who can speak on issues. In the Senate, it is the majority leader.

When a member of Congress is called on to speak, they are told they "have the floor." All representatives present need to pay attention and be respectful when someone has the floor.

The First Congress

The first Congress was held in 1789. It took place in New York City. New York City was the capital of the newly formed United States of America at the time.

Capital or Capitol?

A capital is a city that is the center of government for a county, state, or country. A capitol is a building used for government business. It is where legislators meet. The Capitol is the building in Washington, DC, where the U.S. Congress meets.

Senate chamber, 1937

Who Has the Floor?

With so many jobs to do, Congress needs leaders. Members of each party choose their own leaders. Each leader is called a **floor leader**. In the House, the majority floor leader is an assistant to the speaker. They help manage the debate schedule. One of the perks of being a floor leader is that they often get to talk about a new issue first. This person can control who speaks and try to help their party.

Senator Chuck Schumer (at podium) has served as both majority and minority floor leader.

Whose Desk?

Every senator has their own desk at the Capitol. They are assigned a desk that other senators have used before. Sometimes, a senator will carve their name into the desk drawer to show who sat there!

Senator Mitch McConnell (at podium) has served as both majority and minority floor leader.

The minority floor leader is not an assistant. This person is the main leader of their party in Congress. The minority floor leader has been a member of Congress for a long time. The minority leader gets to speak first for their party. It is tough to be in the minority! Since it has fewer members, the leader needs to be very convincing to get enough votes to win a debate.

In the Senate, the floor leaders are called the majority leader and the minority leader. The majority leader represents the party with the most members in the Senate. The minority leader represents the party with the fewest members in the Senate. Whips are assistant leaders to the majority and minority leaders.

Think and Talk

Why might it be important to have a majority and a minority floor leader?

Whips

When the colonists won their independence from Great Britain, they set out to create a new form of government. They borrowed a word from British Parliament that is still used in Congress. The word is *whip*. Whips serve as assistants to the floor leaders. If a floor leader is not present, the whip takes over until they return. There are whips in both the Senate and the House of Representatives. Each party has its own whip. Whips play an important role. They round up members of their parties to vote for measures in Congress. Whips have the reputation of being very convincing.

Congressional whips help to make deals among members of Congress.

Think and Talk

Why might the author have chosen to include this illustration with the text?

Don't Get Outfoxed!

The word *whip* comes from the British sport of fox chasing. The whip's job was to keep a team of dogs from straying as they chased a wily fox through the countryside.

J. Ham Lewis (left) was Senate whip during the Roosevelt presidency.

Peer Pressure in Congress?

Have you ever had someone use peer pressure to get you to do something? Imagine you are a member of Congress. It seems like everyone in your party wants to vote one way, but you do not agree. You want to follow your own opinion! The whip would apply pressure to get you to vote the same way everyone else in the party is voting. Would it work? Would you follow along with your party? Or would you vote the way you think is best?

Calling All Pages!

Pages in the Senate are usually young people. They often work for a set term while they are in college and are paid a small salary. Pages deliver notes to senators, carry paperwork for them, and prepare meeting spaces, among other things. People as young as 16 may become pages. Pages usually must keep high grades in school.

Before a new issue is brought to the floor, a whip will talk to members of Congress to find out how they feel about it. Will they vote for it? Will there be enough support to win? Many times, the whip can find out if the party will have enough support to win before the vote happens. Sometimes, a whip will try to convince a member of the opposing party to change their mind, too. Whips have been known to work long hours and to make many deals to "whip up" the votes they need to win!

Requests, demands, and peer pressure happen often in Congress, just as they might in your world.

Leaders in the Senate

In today's Senate, there are 100 members. There are two senators from each state. The number 100 is an even number. What if there were a tie vote? Luckily, the Framers thought of this when they wrote the Constitution.

The Constitution lists the laws of the United States. It also lists the duties of its leaders. In the list, there are roles for the vice president. The vice president is second in line for the presidency. The vice president helps carry out the president's goals. The vice president also serves as the president of the Senate. If there is a tie, the vice president is the tiebreaker!

The vice president has other executive responsibilities and does not go to Senate sessions often. When the vice president is not able to be there, a member of the Senate steps in to fill the role.

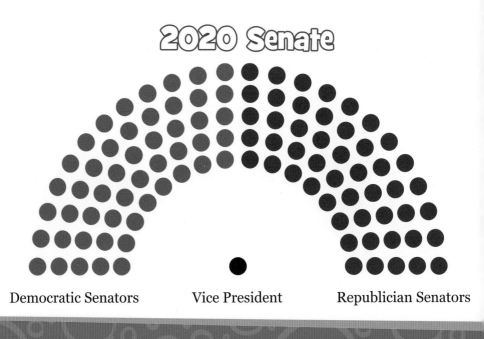

2020 Senate

Democratic Senators   Vice President   Republician Senators

Vice President Kamala Harris

President Pro Tempore

Another key role in the Senate is the president pro tempore. *Pro tempore* is Latin and means "for the time being." Just like it sounds, this is a temporary position. This title is often shortened to *pro tem*. This person is usually a senator from the majority party. They are also the person who has served in the Senate the longest.

The pro tem is like a substitute teacher. They are in charge of carrying out plans and keeping everything in order while the leader is away. Being the pro tem does not carry much responsibility. But they might have one very big job! The pro tem is fourth in line to be president, after the vice president and speaker of the house.

The Senate also has a position that is similar to the speaker of the house. This person is the presiding officer. They are a member of the majority party. This person keeps order during debates, allows people to speak, and follows the rules of the Senate.

It's a Tie! Now What?

John Adams was the first vice president of the United States. He made the tie-breaking vote 29 times during his term!

Presidential Succession

President

Vice President

Speaker of the House of Representatives

President Pro Tempore of the Senate

Secretary of State

Secretary of Defense

Attorney General

There is an official line of presidential succession in place. It is there in case the president dies while in office or is unable to do the job.

A Congress for the People

The United States is a proud democracy. Citizens vote for the people they think will do the best job to represent their needs. The Constitution gives rights to all Americans.

Congress is a diverse group of people from all 50 states. There are also non-voting members representing Washington, DC and the U.S. territories. The members are meant to work together to make laws. They should also work to protect the rights outlined in the Constitution.

Much like a team, members of Congress need to work together to succeed. They are meant to choose leaders who will help Congress stay organized, be informed, and run smoothly. The speaker of the house, floor leaders, whips, and the president pro tempore each play a unique role. Each role is vital to meet Congress's goals each session. These leaders make the United States Congress the strong governing force it is today.

The 117th Congress

In 2021, the 117th Congress was sworn in. It was the most diverse Congress in the history of the United States.

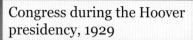
Congress during the Hoover presidency, 1929

Think and Talk

What do you notice about Congress 100 years ago that seems different from the Congress of today?

Glossary

bicameral—having two parts

Capitol—the building in Washington, DC, in which the Senate and House of Representatives meet

Congress—the legislative branch of the United States government, made up of the House of Representatives and the Senate

democracy—a form of government in which citizens elect their leaders by voting

floor leader—a member of Congress chosen by a party to take charge of its organization and strategy on the floor

House of Representatives—part of the U.S. legislative branch, made up of elected people from each of the 50 states

legislative branch—the division of the United States government that is responsible for making laws, known as Congress

majority—the group or party that is the greater part of a large group

minority—the group or party that is the smaller part of a larger group

Senate—part of the United States legislative branch, made up of two elected people from each of the 50 states

senators—elected members of the United States Senate

speaker of the house—a member of the majority party nominated to provide leadership in the House of Representatives

Index

Civics in Action

Congress makes the laws and represents the people. A representative is there to serve the people's interests. The people may be able to influence what the representatives do in Congress. There are no guarantees that the representatives will do what the people ask, but the more people they hear from, the more likely they are to act!

1. Choose an issue or problem you care about.

2. Research that issue.

3. Write a short speech you might present to a Congressional representative.

4. Present your speech to the class.